AMAZING INVENTIONS

CELL PHONES AND SMARTPHONES

A GRAPHIC HISTORY

8:12
THURS SEPT 24

60°F

hey, u around ?

Calling work

BLAKE HOENA

ILLUSTRATED BY **CEEJ ROWLAND**

Graphic Universe™ • Minneapolis

Graphic Universe™
An imprint of Lerner Publishing Group, Inc.
241 First Avenue North
Minneapolis, MN 55401 USA

For reading levels and more information, look up this title at www.lernerbooks.com.

Main body text set in CCHedgeBackwards 7/9
Typeface provided by Comicraft.

Library of Congress Cataloging-in-Publication Data

Names: Hoena, B. A., writer. | Rowland, Ceej, illustrator.
Title: Cell phones and smartphones : a graphic history / written by Blake Hoena ; illustrated by Ceej Rowland.
Description: Minneapolis : Graphic Universe, [2021] | Series: Amazing inventions | Includes bibliographical references and index. | Audience: Ages 8–12 | Audience: Grades 4–6 | Summary: "Cell phones allowed people to connect on the go, and smartphones have transformed the way we share information. Discover the landmark shifts in phone technology-and the people-that have shaped modern communication"— Provided by publisher.
Identifiers: LCCN 2020006417 (print) | LCCN 2020006418 (ebook) | ISBN 9781541581494 (library binding) | ISBN 9781728417455 (ebook)
Subjects: LCSH: Cell phones—Juvenile literature. | Cell phones—Comic books, strips, etc. | Smartphones—Juvenile literature. | Smartphones—Comic books, strips, etc.
Classification: LCC TK6564.4.C4 H64 2021 (print) | LCC TK6564.4.C4 (ebook) | DDC 621.3845/6—dc23

LC record available at https://lccn.loc.gov/2020006417
LC ebook record available at https://lccn.loc.gov/2020006418

Manufactured in the United States of America
1 - 47332 - 47959 - 2/1/2021

TABLE OF CONTENTS

CHAPTER 1
MAKING CONNECTIONS

SMARTPHONES ARE OUR CONSTANT SIDEKICKS! IT IS HARD TO IMAGINE LIFE WITHOUT THEM. THESE DEVICES CONNECT US WITH CONTENT AND COMMUNITIES AROUND THE WORLD. THEY HELP US LEARN, EXPLORE, GAME, AND SO MUCH MORE.

IS THAT A NEW GAME?

NO, I'M DOING RESEARCH FOR A SCHOOL PAPER.

CHECK THIS OUT. THAT'S WHAT PHONES USED TO LOOK LIKE.

WEIRD. IT DOESN'T EVEN HAVE A TOUCH SCREEN!

BUT PHONES DID NOT ALWAYS HAVE SUCH AN IMPACT ON PEOPLE'S LIVES.

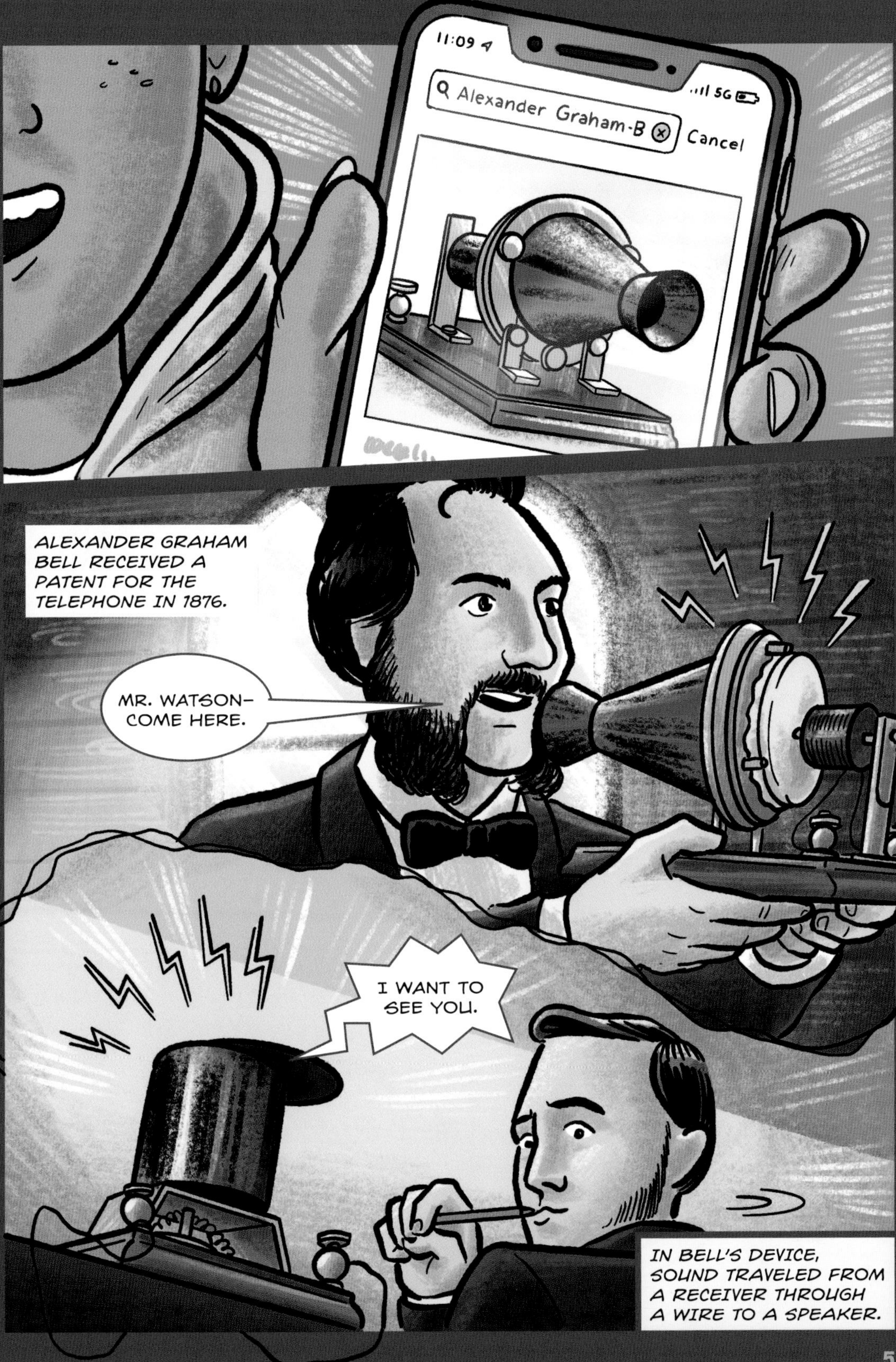
11:09
5G
Alexander Graham-B
Cancel
ALEXANDER GRAHAM BELL RECEIVED A PATENT FOR THE TELEPHONE IN 1876.
MR. WATSON— COME HERE.
I WANT TO SEE YOU.
IN BELL'S DEVICE, SOUND TRAVELED FROM A RECEIVER THROUGH A WIRE TO A SPEAKER.

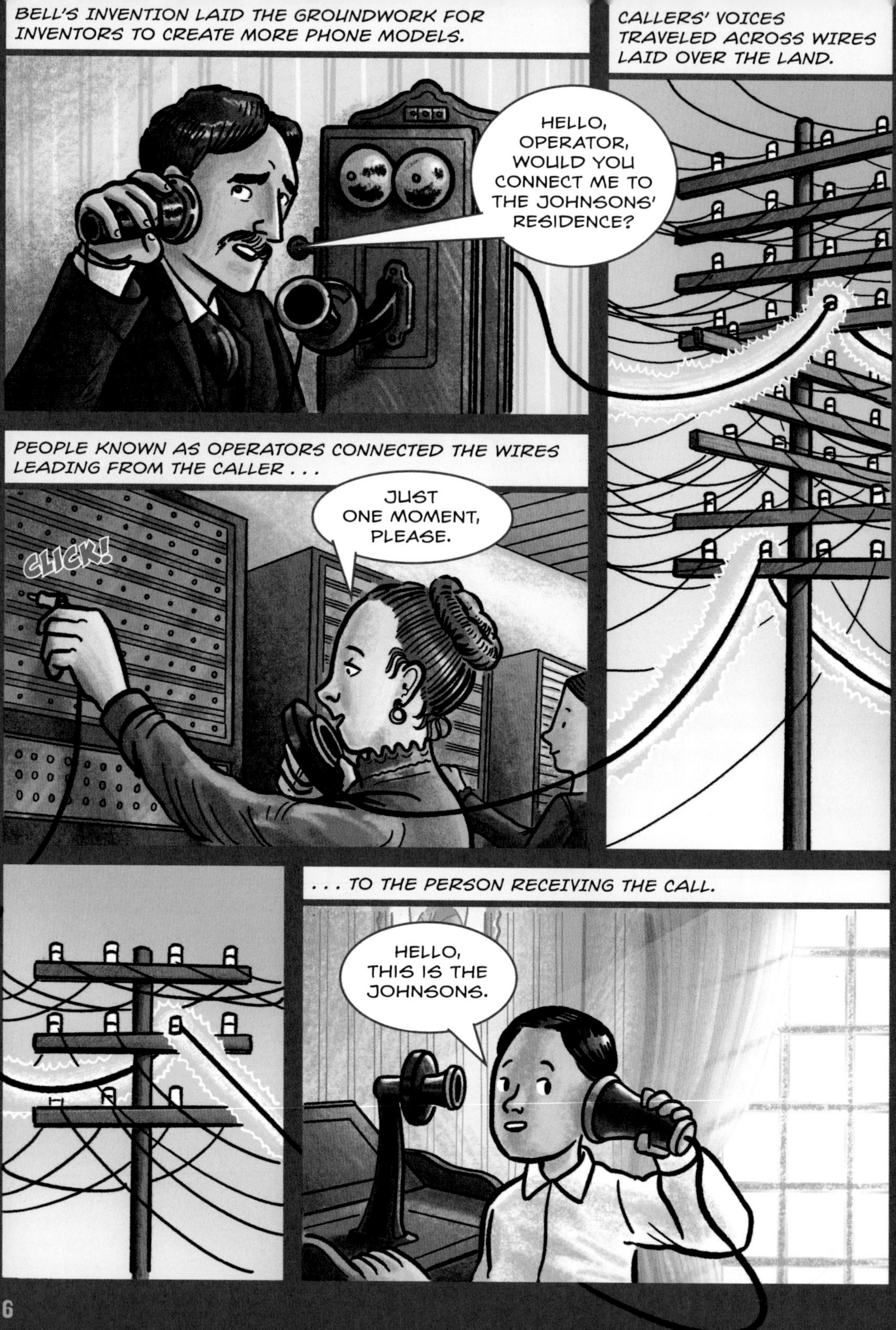
BELL'S INVENTION LAID THE GROUNDWORK FOR INVENTORS TO CREATE MORE PHONE MODELS.
HELLO, OPERATOR, WOULD YOU CONNECT ME TO THE JOHNSONS' RESIDENCE?
CALLERS' VOICES TRAVELED ACROSS WIRES LAID OVER THE LAND.
PEOPLE KNOWN AS OPERATORS CONNECTED THE WIRES LEADING FROM THE CALLER . . .
JUST ONE MOMENT, PLEASE.
CLICK!
. . . TO THE PERSON RECEIVING THE CALL.
HELLO, THIS IS THE JOHNSONS.

In 1900, Reginald Aubrey Fessenden of Canada invented a device that could transmit the human voice through radio waves rather than wires.

FESSENDEN'S INVENTION LED TO EARLY WIRELESS COMMUNICATION DEVICES.

IN THE MID-1920S, GERMANY'S NATIONAL TRAIN SYSTEM OFFERED A WIRELESS RADIO TELEPHONE SERVICE TO FIRST-CLASS PASSENGERS.

DURING WORLD WAR II (1939-1945), US ARMY SOLDIERS USED RADIO TELEPHONES TO COMMUNICATE IN THE FIELD.

HALLO, WIE GEHT ES DIR?

WE'RE PINNED DOWN BY ENEMY ARTILLERY. OVER.

IN THE MID-1940S, THE AMERICAN TELEPHONE & TELEGRAPH COMPANY (AT&T), FORMED BY THE BELL SYSTEM COMPANY, INTRODUCED ITS MOBILE TELEPHONE SERVICE. IT ALLOWED RADIO COMMUNICATION FROM AUTOMOBILES.

HOW MUCH DOES THIS THING WEIGH?

ABOUT EIGHTY POUNDS.

ALL OF THESE DEVICES WORKED MORE LIKE TWO-WAY RADIOS THAN MODERN CELL PHONES. ONLY ONE PERSON ON THE CALL COULD TALK AT A TIME.

THE MOBILE TELEPHONE SERVICE NETWORK HAD A SINGLE BASE STATION TOWER. THIS MEANT IT COULD NOT HANDLE MANY CALLS AT THE SAME TIME. IN THE LATE 1940s, WILLIAM RAE YOUNG, ENGINEER FOR BELL LABS, THOUGHT OF A SOLUTION. HE SHARED IT WITH HIS BOSS, DOUGLAS H. RING.

INSTEAD OF USING ONE TOWER AS A BASE STATION, WHAT IF WE SET UP A SERIES OF TOWERS?

HOW WOULD THIS WORK?

AS A CALLER MOVES ACROSS THE NETWORK, ONE TOWER WILL HAND OFF THE CALL TO THE NEXT TOWER.

THEN *THAT* TOWER WILL TRANSMIT THE CALL. THIS BROADENS THE RANGE OF THE NETWORK.

EACH TOWER'S RANGE COVERED A PORTION, OR CELL, OF THE NETWORK. YOUNG HAD PROPOSED THE FIRST CELLULAR NETWORK.

AT&T WORKED ON YOUNG'S IDEA. IT ALSO CONTINUED TO DEVELOP OTHER INNOVATIONS. IN 1964, IT RELEASED THE IMPROVED MOBILE TELEPHONE SERVICE (IMTS). UNLIKE PREVIOUS SYSTEMS, THE IMTS DID NOT NEED AN OPERATOR. IT ALSO ALLOWED PEOPLE ON BOTH ENDS OF A CALL TO TALK AT THE SAME TIME!

CHAPTER 2
EARLY MOBILE PHONES

WE'RE JUST HEADING TO MEET WITH A NEW CLIENT.

DURING THE 1950S AND 1960S, COMPANIES LIKE GENERAL ELECTRIC AND MOTOROLA HAD DEVELOPED SMALLER AND LIGHTER MOBILE PHONES.

BUT THE MOBILE PHONES HAD A HIGH COST. MOST USERS WERE SALESPEOPLE OR BUSINESSPEOPLE.

TWO-WAY RADIO

BATTERY & RELAY ASSEMBLY

AROUND THIS TIME, PEOPLE BEGAN CALLING THESE PHONES "CAR PHONES." THE DEVICES WERE TOO BIG AND BULKY FOR A PERSON TO CARRY AROUND, BUT THEY WORKED WELL IN A CAR.

BY THE LATE 1960S, BELL LABS ENGINEERS BEGAN ACTING ON WILLIAM RAE YOUNG'S IDEA. THEY PUT UP TOWERS TO CREATE A CELLULAR NETWORK.

JOEL, THIS IS MARTY. I'M CALLING YOU FROM A CELL PHONE . . .

BUT A RIVAL, MOTOROLA, ENDED UP BEING THE FIRST TO DEVELOP A TRULY MOBILE PHONE THAT COULD UTILIZE THE NEW NETWORK. ON APRIL 3, 1973, ENGINEER MARTIN COOPER MADE A CALL ON THE NETWORK USING MOTOROLA'S DYNAMIC ADAPTIVE TOTAL AREA COVERAGE (DYNATAC) PHONE. A JOURNALIST WITNESSED THE CALL.

WHO DID COOPER DIAL FOR THIS HISTORIC MOMENT? JOEL ENGEL, HEAD OF BELL LABS. COOPER BRAGGED TO ENGEL ABOUT MOTOROLA'S NEW INVENTION.

. . . A REAL HANDHELD PORTABLE CELL PHONE.

ENGEL

THE PHONE COOPER USED WAS JUST A PROTOTYPE. MOTOROLA TOOK ANOTHER TEN YEARS TO PRODUCE THE DYNATAC 8000X FOR COMMERCIAL USE. THE DEVICE WAS EXPENSIVE AND BULKY.

HEIGHT: 13"
DEPTH: 3.5"
WIDTH: 1.75"
WEIGHT: 1.75 LBS.

PRICE: $3,995.00

BATTERY LIFE: 30 MINUTES OF TALK TIME BEFORE RECHARGING

BECAUSE OF ITS SIZE, THE CELL PHONE EARNED THE NICKNAME THE "BRICK."

THAT SAME YEAR, 1983, AMERITECH CORPORATION ROLLED OUT THE FIRST GENERATION (1G) CELLULAR NETWORK IN THE UNITED STATES. OTHER TELECOMMUNICATIONS COMPANIES SOON FOLLOWED WITH THEIR OWN 1G NETWORKS.

1G NETWORKS HAD POOR SOUND QUALITY. BUT PAIRED WITH MOTOROLA'S DYNATAC, THEY MADE EVERYDAY WIRELESS CALLING A REALITY—FOR THOSE WHO COULD AFFORD IT.

TECHNOLOGY COMPANIES CONTINUED TO MAKE CELL PHONES SMALLER, LIGHTER, AND LESS EXPENSIVE. THROUGHOUT MUCH OF THE 1980S, MOTOROLA LED THE WAY. IN 1989, IT RELEASED THE MICROTAC 9800X.

OKAY, I GOTTA GO. LATER.

CLICK!

IT WAS THE FIRST FLIP PHONE, WITH A MOUTHPIECE THAT FOLDED OVER THE KEYPAD. THIS MADE THE PHONE MUCH SMALLER THAN EARLIER MODELS.

MOTOROLA ADVERTISED IT AS A POCKET CELLULAR TELEPHONE. PEOPLE COULD MORE EASILY CARRY THE PHONE AROUND. BUT THE MICROTAC 9800X STILL COST A LOT OF MONEY. IT SOLD FOR BETWEEN $2,500 AND $3,500.

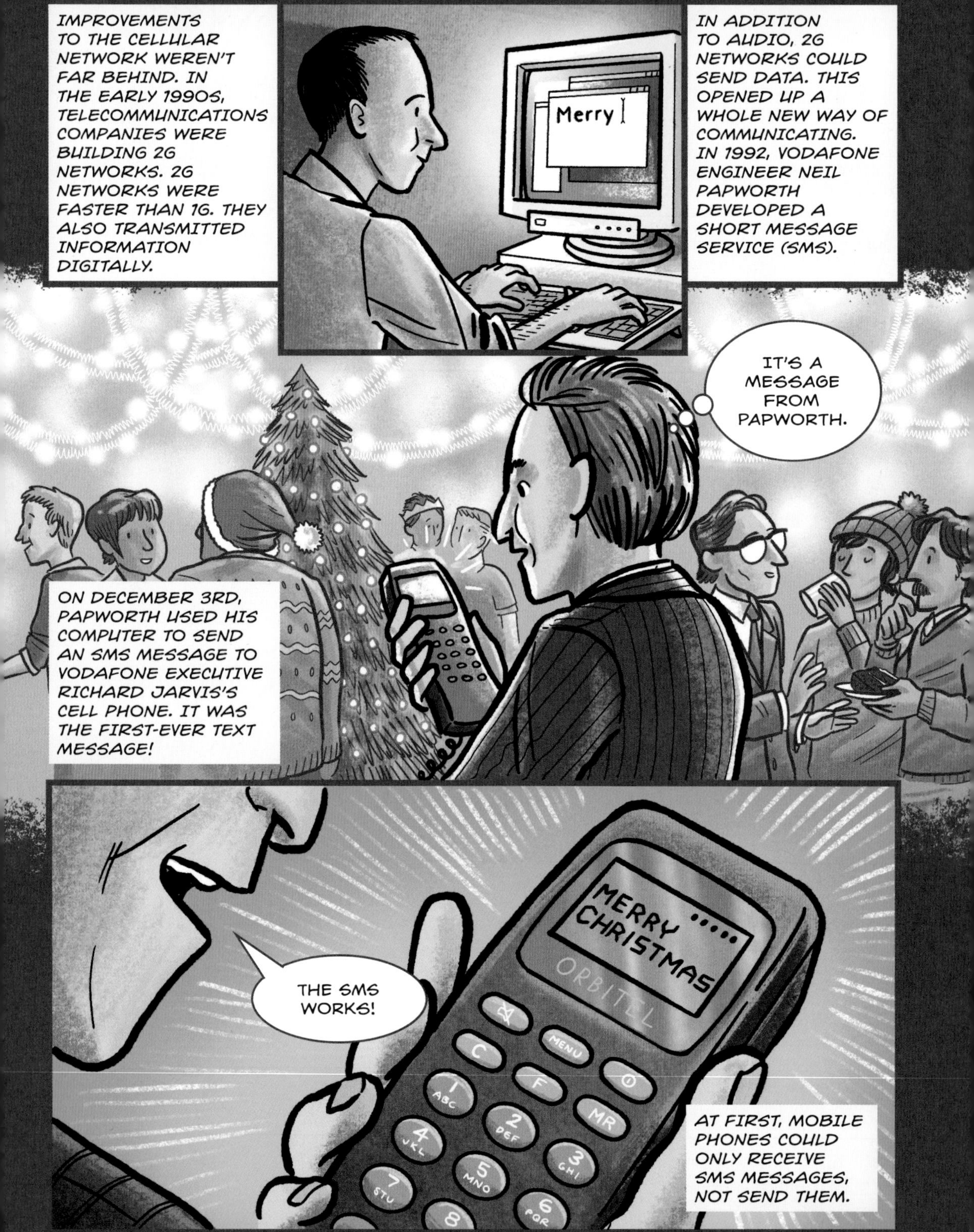
IMPROVEMENTS TO THE CELLULAR NETWORK WEREN'T FAR BEHIND. IN THE EARLY 1990S, TELECOMMUNICATIONS COMPANIES WERE BUILDING 2G NETWORKS. 2G NETWORKS WERE FASTER THAN 1G. THEY ALSO TRANSMITTED INFORMATION DIGITALLY.
Merry
IN ADDITION TO AUDIO, 2G NETWORKS COULD SEND DATA. THIS OPENED UP A WHOLE NEW WAY OF COMMUNICATING. IN 1992, VODAFONE ENGINEER NEIL PAPWORTH DEVELOPED A SHORT MESSAGE SERVICE (SMS).
IT'S A MESSAGE FROM PAPWORTH.
ON DECEMBER 3RD, PAPWORTH USED HIS COMPUTER TO SEND AN SMS MESSAGE TO VODAFONE EXECUTIVE RICHARD JARVIS'S CELL PHONE. IT WAS THE FIRST-EVER TEXT MESSAGE!
MERRY CHRISTMAS
ORBITEL
THE SMS WORKS!
AT FIRST, MOBILE PHONES COULD ONLY RECEIVE SMS MESSAGES, NOT SEND THEM.

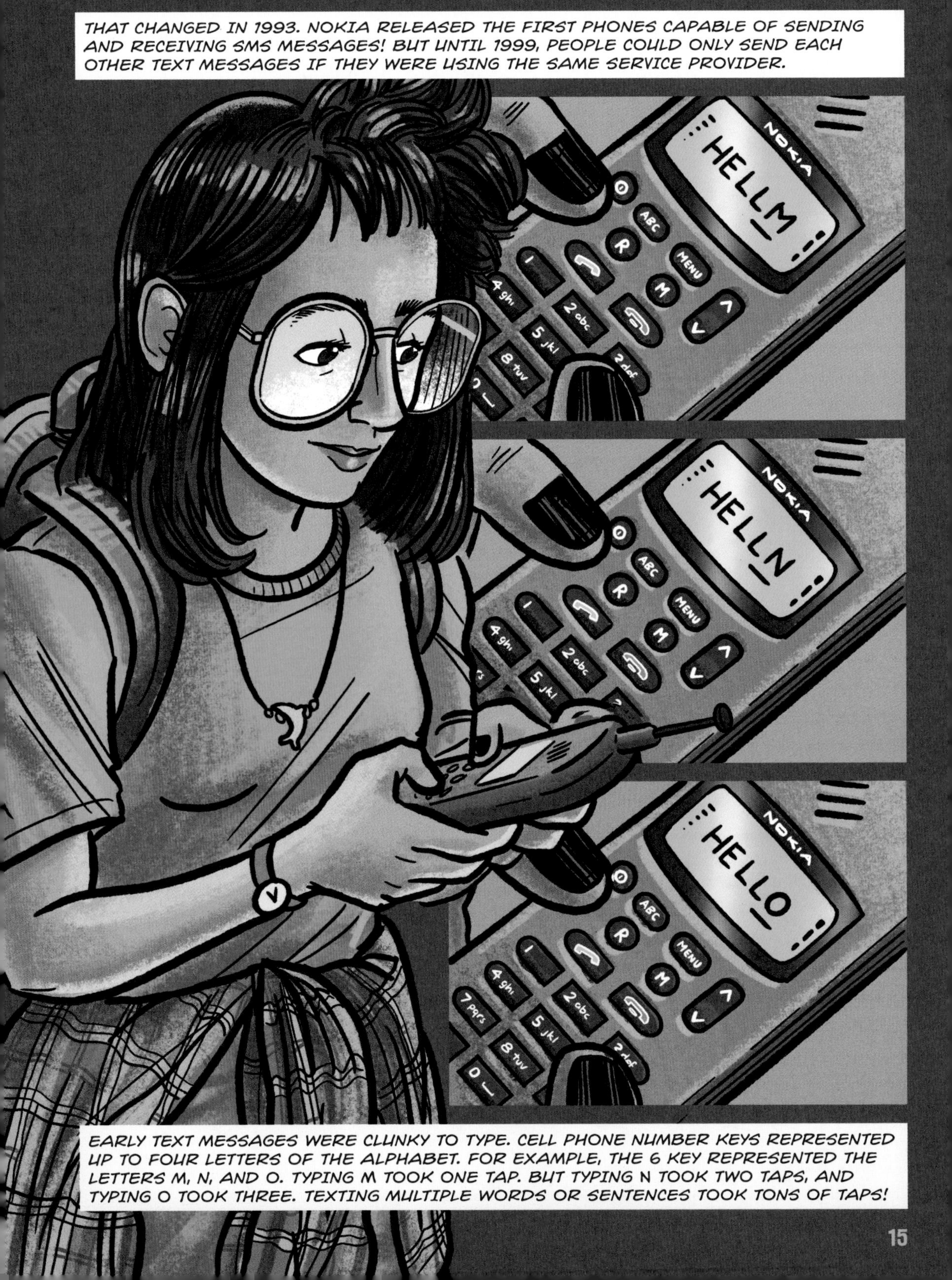
THAT CHANGED IN 1993. NOKIA RELEASED THE FIRST PHONES CAPABLE OF SENDING AND RECEIVING SMS MESSAGES! BUT UNTIL 1999, PEOPLE COULD ONLY SEND EACH OTHER TEXT MESSAGES IF THEY WERE USING THE SAME SERVICE PROVIDER.
NOKIA
HELLM
NOKIA
HELLN
NOKIA
HELLO
EARLY TEXT MESSAGES WERE CLUNKY TO TYPE. CELL PHONE NUMBER KEYS REPRESENTED UP TO FOUR LETTERS OF THE ALPHABET. FOR EXAMPLE, THE 6 KEY REPRESENTED THE LETTERS M, N, AND O. TYPING M TOOK ONE TAP. BUT TYPING N TOOK TWO TAPS, AND TYPING O TOOK THREE. TEXTING MULTIPLE WORDS OR SENTENCES TOOK TONS OF TAPS!

CHAPTER 3
PHONES GET SMART

CELL PHONES CONTINUED TO GAIN FEATURES THROUGHOUT THE 1990S. IN 1994, COMPUTER COMPANY IBM RELEASED THE ADVANCED CELL PHONE SIMON.

IT HAD A CALENDAR AND A CALCULATOR. IT COULD SEND AND RECEIVE EMAILS. IT EVEN HAD A TOUCH SCREEN! PEOPLE COULD USE A STYLUS TO QUICKLY TAP KEYS, DRAW, AND MORE.

SIMON ALSO HAD THE FIRST MOBILE PHONE GAME, SCRAMBLE.

I WIN AGAIN!

MANY PEOPLE CONSIDER SIMON THE WORLD'S FIRST SMARTPHONE.

BUT THE DEVICE WAS NOT IN HIGH DEMAND DUE TO ITS SIZE. SIMON WAS EIGHT INCHES TALL—SEVERAL INCHES LONGER THAN OTHER MOBILE PHONES. SMALLER PORTABLE PHONES WERE MORE POPULAR.

ONE WAS THE MOTOROLA STARTAC, RELEASED IN 1996. THE DEVICE WAS JUST UNDER FOUR INCHES LONG.

IT WAS ALSO THE FIRST CLAMSHELL PHONE. THIS DESIGN FOLDED COMPLETELY IN HALF.

THAT SAME YEAR, NOKIA INTRODUCED ITS 8110 PHONE. IT HAD AN INTERNAL ANTENNA, THE FIRST OF ITS KIND RELEASED IN THE UNITED STATES.

IN 1997, GERMAN COMPANY SIEMENS RELEASED THE S10. THIS WAS THE FIRST MOBILE PHONE TO HAVE A COLOR SCREEN.

IN 1997, THE NOKIA 9000 COMMUNICATOR DEBUTED. IT FLIPPED ON ITS SIDE, OPENING TO A LARGE DISPLAY SCREEN. IT COULD ALSO ACCESS THE INTERNET! THIS OPENED A WHOLE NEW MOBILE PHONE WORLD. THE TERM "SMARTPHONE" CAME INTO USE AROUND THIS TIME, INSPIRED BY MOBILE PHONES WITH INTERNET ACCESS.

IN 1999, NOKIA RELEASED THE 7110. IT WAS THE FIRST MOBILE PHONE WITH A WEB BROWSER.

MEANWHILE, TECH COMPANIES WERE CREATING 3G NETWORKS FOR THESE MORE ADVANCED PHONES.

THE GLOBAL POSITIONING SYSTEM (GPS) WAS ANOTHER IMPORTANT CELL PHONE DEVELOPMENT. GPS IS A SYSTEM OF SATELLITES THAT TELLS PEOPLE EXACTLY WHERE THEY ARE ON EARTH AND PROVIDES NAVIGATIONAL DIRECTIONS. THE BENEFON ESC! WAS THE FIRST CELL PHONE TO USE THIS SYSTEM.

WHICH WAY SHOULD WE GO?

IT SAYS OUR HOTEL IS THAT WAY.

HOTEL

BENEFON

IN 2001, JAPANESE ELECTRONICS MAKER SHARP RELEASED THE J-SH04. IT WAS THE FIRST MOBILE PHONE WITH A BUILT-IN CAMERA. IT ALLOWED USERS TO TAKE AND SEND PHOTOS ON THEIR PHONES!

SMILE!

J-PHONE

THE PHONE HAD A CAMERA LENS ON THE BACK AND A COLOR SCREEN ON THE FRONT. THE J-SH04 ALSO HAD INTERNET ACCESS, SO PEOPLE COULD EMAIL PHOTOS THEY TOOK ON THE PHONE.

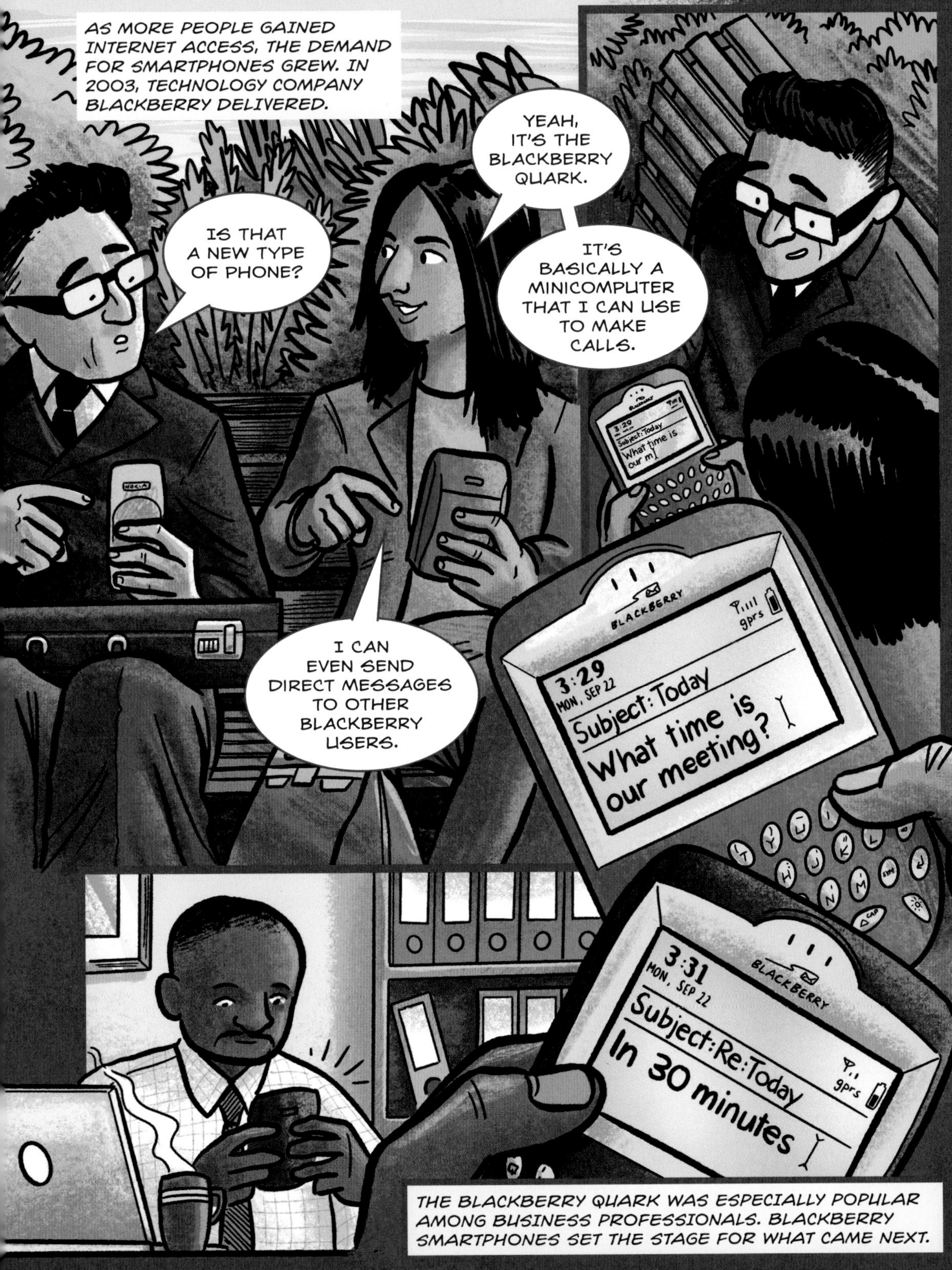
AS MORE PEOPLE GAINED INTERNET ACCESS, THE DEMAND FOR SMARTPHONES GREW. IN 2003, TECHNOLOGY COMPANY BLACKBERRY DELIVERED.
IS THAT A NEW TYPE OF PHONE?
YEAH, IT'S THE BLACKBERRY QUARK.
IT'S BASICALLY A MINICOMPUTER THAT I CAN USE TO MAKE CALLS.
I CAN EVEN SEND DIRECT MESSAGES TO OTHER BLACKBERRY USERS.
BLACKBERRY
gprs
3:29
MON, SEP 22
Subject: Today
What time is our meeting?
3:31
MON, SEP 22
BLACKBERRY
Subject:Re:Today
gprs
In 30 minutes
THE BLACKBERRY QUARK WAS ESPECIALLY POPULAR AMONG BUSINESS PROFESSIONALS. BLACKBERRY SMARTPHONES SET THE STAGE FOR WHAT CAME NEXT.

CHAPTER 4
PART PHONE, PART COMPUTER

BLACKBERRY HAD TAKEN THE MOBILE WORLD BY STORM. BUT ANOTHER COMPANY WAS ABOUT TO CREATE A MOBILE-PHONE REVOLUTION.

IN 2001, APPLE COMPUTER, INC. HAD RELEASED ITS HIGHLY POPULAR IPOD. THIS DEVICE CHANGED THE WAY PEOPLE PURCHASED AND LISTENED TO MUSIC. NEXT, APPLE CO-FOUNDER AND CEO STEVE JOBS SET HIS SIGHTS ON THE MOBILE PHONE MARKET.

Think different.

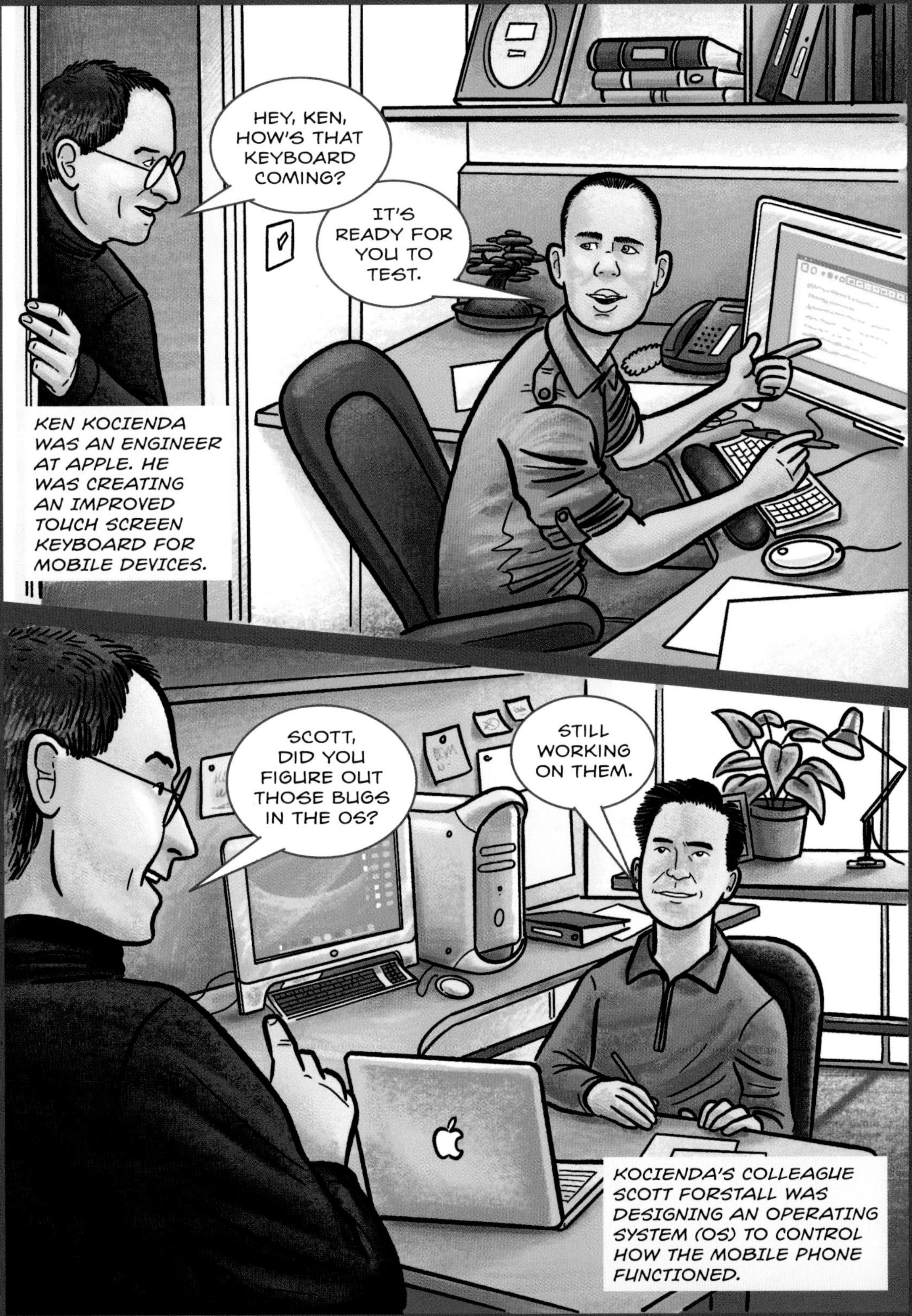

KEN KOCIENDA WAS AN ENGINEER AT APPLE. HE WAS CREATING AN IMPROVED TOUCH SCREEN KEYBOARD FOR MOBILE DEVICES.
HEY, KEN, HOW'S THAT KEYBOARD COMING?
IT'S READY FOR YOU TO TEST.
SCOTT, DID YOU FIGURE OUT THOSE BUGS IN THE OS?
STILL WORKING ON THEM.
KOCIENDA'S COLLEAGUE SCOTT FORSTALL WAS DESIGNING AN OPERATING SYSTEM (OS) TO CONTROL HOW THE MOBILE PHONE FUNCTIONED.

IN JANUARY 2007, JOBS WAS READY TO REVEAL HIS TEAM'S HARD WORK.

WHAT WE WANT TO DO IS MAKE A LEAPFROG PRODUCT THAT IS WAY SMARTER THAN ANY MOBILE DEVICE THAT'S EVER BEEN AND SUPER EASY TO USE. THIS IS WHAT IPHONE IS.

THE PHONE JOBS INTRODUCED HAD A TOUCH SCREEN ON THE FRONT . . .

WE'RE GONNA REINVENT THE PHONE . . . WITH A REVOLUTIONARY USER INTERFACE.

WE HAVE INVENTED A NEW TECHNOLOGY CALLED MULTI TOUCH.

WE'VE GOT A TWO-MEGAPIXEL CAMERA BUILT RIGHT IN.

. . . AND AN ADVANCED CAMERA ON THE BACK.

BUT THE IPHONE'S OS WAS ITS MOST IMPRESSIVE FEATURE. IT COULD RUN PROGRAMS, CALLED APPLICATIONS, SIMILAR TO A DESKTOP COMPUTER! ONE OF THE MOST POPULAR WAS ITUNES, WHICH STORED AND PLAYED MUSIC THE SAME WAY IT DID ON THE IPOD.

THE IPHONE ADVANCED THE ERA OF MOBILE COMPUTING.

CHECK THIS OUT. IT HAS A WEB BROWSER, APPS . . . I CAN EVEN WATCH VIDEOS ON YOUTUBE!

THE IPHONE QUICKLY BECAME ONE OF THE WORLD'S BEST-SELLING DEVICES.

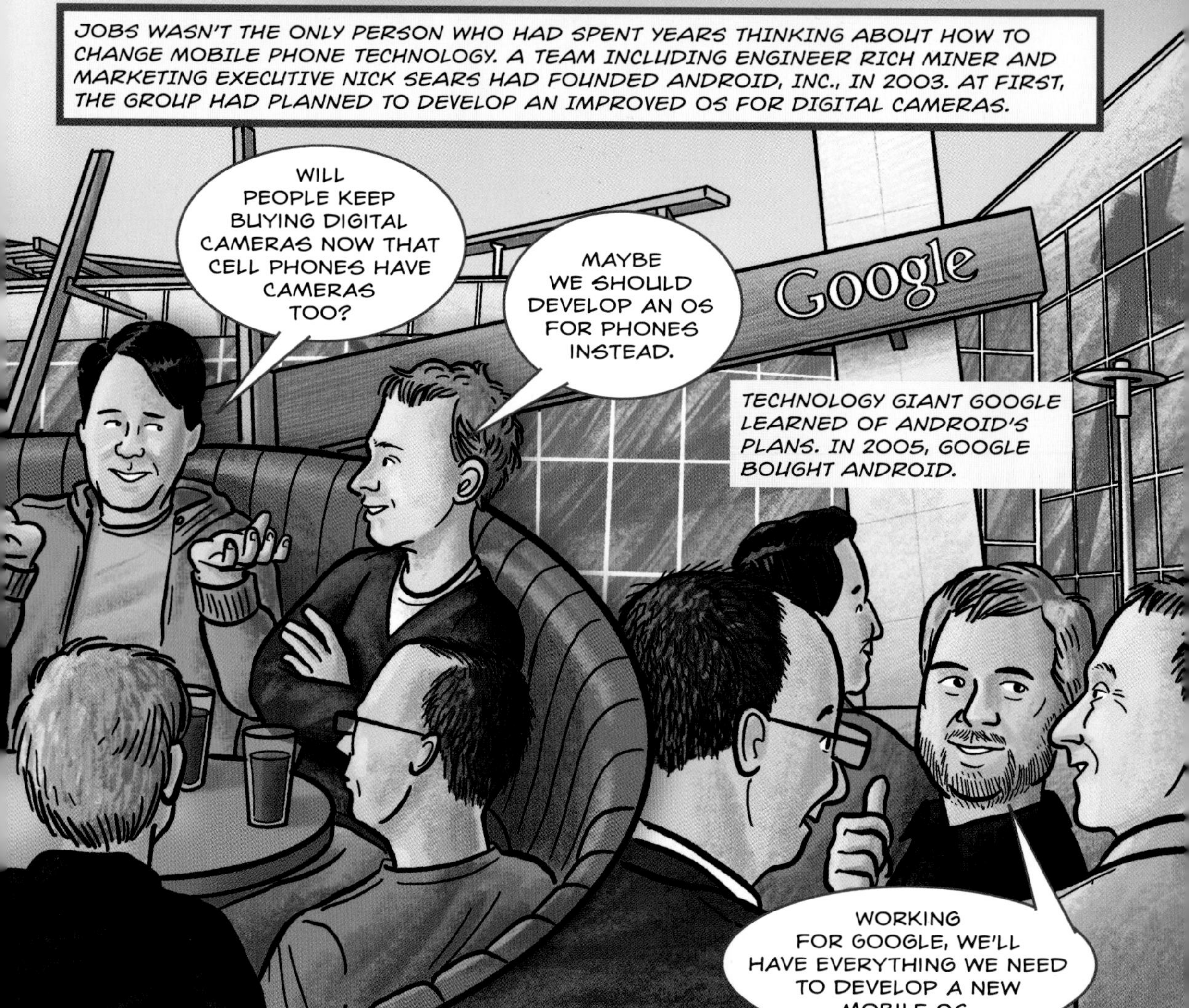

JOBS WASN'T THE ONLY PERSON WHO HAD SPENT YEARS THINKING ABOUT HOW TO CHANGE MOBILE PHONE TECHNOLOGY. A TEAM INCLUDING ENGINEER RICH MINER AND MARKETING EXECUTIVE NICK SEARS HAD FOUNDED ANDROID, INC., IN 2003. AT FIRST, THE GROUP HAD PLANNED TO DEVELOP AN IMPROVED OS FOR DIGITAL CAMERAS.
WILL PEOPLE KEEP BUYING DIGITAL CAMERAS NOW THAT CELL PHONES HAVE CAMERAS TOO?
MAYBE WE SHOULD DEVELOP AN OS FOR PHONES INSTEAD.
Google
TECHNOLOGY GIANT GOOGLE LEARNED OF ANDROID'S PLANS. IN 2005, GOOGLE BOUGHT ANDROID.
WORKING FOR GOOGLE, WE'LL HAVE EVERYTHING WE NEED TO DEVELOP A NEW MOBILE OS.

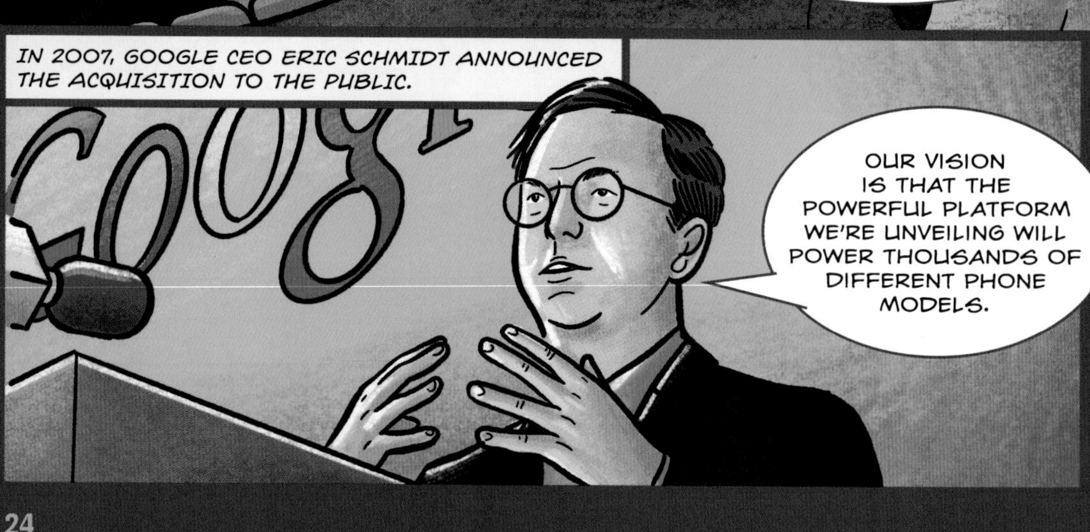

IN 2007, GOOGLE CEO ERIC SCHMIDT ANNOUNCED THE ACQUISITION TO THE PUBLIC.
OUR VISION IS THAT THE POWERFUL PLATFORM WE'RE UNVEILING WILL POWER THOUSANDS OF DIFFERENT PHONE MODELS.

GOOGLE COLLABORATED WITH CELL PHONE COMPANY T-MOBILE, WHICH BUILT A DEVICE TO RUN THE ANDROID OS. THE T-MOBILE G1, RELEASED IN 2008, WAS THE FIRST ANDROID PHONE.

THE T-MOBILE G1 HAD MANY FEATURES SIMILAR TO THOSE OF THE IPHONE. APPLE SUDDENLY FACED SERIOUS COMPETITION.

UNLIKE APPLE'S OS, WHICH ONLY OPERATED ON IPHONES, ANDROID RAN ON MANY DIFFERENT PHONES MADE BY MANY COMPANIES. OVER THE NEXT FEW YEARS, SEVERAL COMPANIES DEVELOPED ANDROID SMARTPHONES.

THIS IS THE NEW GALAXY S.

I HEAR IT HAS AN ON-SCREEN KEYBOARD JUST LIKE THE IPHONE.

YOU CAN ALSO UPLOAD VIDEOS DIRECTLY TO YOUTUBE.

ONE ANDROID PHONE STOOD OUT FROM THE OTHERS. THE SAMSUNG GALAXY SERIES ARRIVED IN 2009. THE SERIES BECAME IPHONE'S STRONGEST COMPETITOR.

APPLE AND ANDROID CONTINUED TO UPDATE THEIR OPERATING SYSTEMS AND PHONES. DESIGNS GREW SLEEKER, PROCESSORS FASTER, AND CAMERAS MORE ADVANCED. THE COMPANIES ALSO DEVELOPED NEW FEATURES.

IS EVERYTHING OKAY, HON?

YEAH, I'M JUST STUCK ON A MATH PROBLEM.

LET ME SEE!

IN 2010, APPLE DEBUTED FACETIME. THIS APP ALLOWED VIDEO CALLS BETWEEN APPLE USERS.

VIDEO-CHATTING APPS FOR THE ANDROID OS BECAME AVAILABLE THE SAME YEAR.

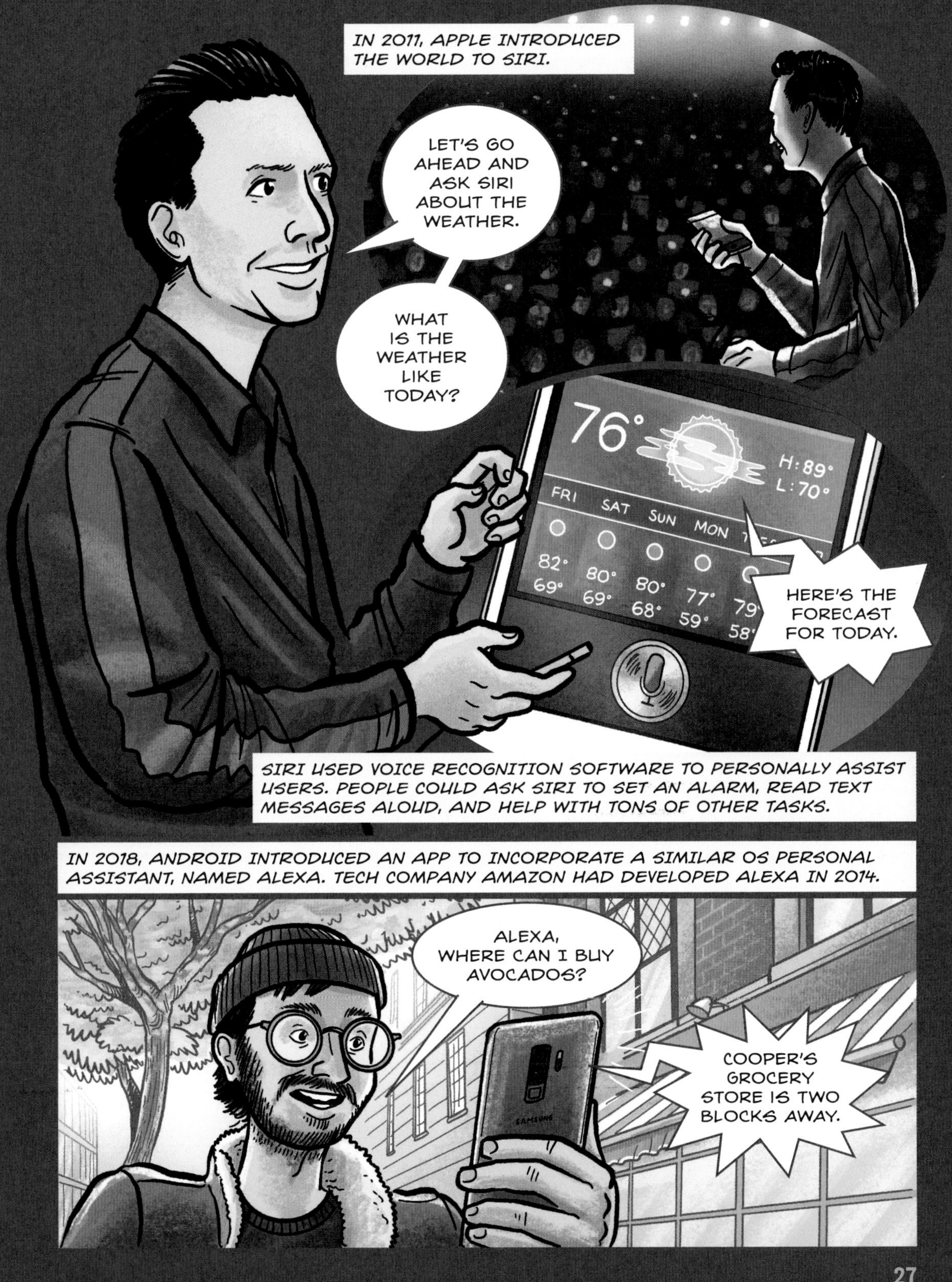
IN 2011, APPLE INTRODUCED THE WORLD TO SIRI.
LET'S GO AHEAD AND ASK SIRI ABOUT THE WEATHER.
WHAT IS THE WEATHER LIKE TODAY?
76°
H:89°
L:70°
FRI SAT SUN MON
82° 69° 80° 69° 80° 68° 77° 59°
HERE'S THE FORECAST FOR TODAY.
SIRI USED VOICE RECOGNITION SOFTWARE TO PERSONALLY ASSIST USERS. PEOPLE COULD ASK SIRI TO SET AN ALARM, READ TEXT MESSAGES ALOUD, AND HELP WITH TONS OF OTHER TASKS.
IN 2018, ANDROID INTRODUCED AN APP TO INCORPORATE A SIMILAR OS PERSONAL ASSISTANT, NAMED ALEXA. TECH COMPANY AMAZON HAD DEVELOPED ALEXA IN 2014.
ALEXA, WHERE CAN I BUY AVOCADOS?
COOPER'S GROCERY STORE IS TWO BLOCKS AWAY.

ADVANCEMENTS IN SMARTPHONE TECHNOLOGY CONTINUED. TECH COMPANIES CREATED PHONES WITH BIGGER, SHARPER SCREENS FOR PLAYING GAMES AND WATCHING VIDEOS.

THE 2019 GALAXY FOLD UNFOLDED TO REVEAL A 7.3-INCH SCREEN!

IMPROVED CAMERAS AND NEW IMAGE RECOGNITION APPS HELPED USERS CONNECT WITH EVERYTHING AROUND THEM.

MONARCH BUTTERFLY.

THESE ADVANCES LED TO THE DEBUT OF AUGMENTED REALITY GAMES.

THAT IS A FOUNTAIN OF HEALING.

GOOD, I GOT BANGED UP AFTER THAT LAST ENCOUNTER.

IN THE FUTURE, PHONES MAY NOT EVEN BE OUR GO-TO SMART TOOLS. WEARABLES SUCH AS SMART WATCHES HAVE MANY OF THE SAME FUNCTIONS. DEVELOPERS ARE IMPROVING THESE DEVICES EVERY DAY.

WHEN ARE YOU GOING TO BE HOME?

I'M JUST ABOUT DONE WITH MY WORKOUT.

THE FIRST TELEPHONES HAD A SINGLE PURPOSE. THEY HELPED PEOPLE COMMUNICATE OVER LONG DISTANCES. SINCE THEN, PHONES HAVE TAKEN US FAR BEYOND SIMPLE COMMUNICATION. THEY HAVE BECOME MINICOMPUTERS WITH A WIDER REACH THAN EVER, KEEPING US CONNECTED TO THE WHOLE WORLD.

SOURCE NOTES

PAGE 5

Leonard C. Bruno, "'Mr. Watson, Come Here': First Release of Bell Papers Goes Online," Library of Congress, April 1999, https://www .loc.gov/loc/lcib/9904/bell.html.

PAGE 6

Charles Enman, "One Against the World," *The Ottawa Citizen*, September 13, 1999, https://www.ieee.ca/millennium/radio /radio_world.html.

PAGE 10

Larry Seltzer, "Cell Phone Inventor Talks of First Cell Call," InformationWeek, April 3, 2013, https://www.informationweek.com/wireless /cell-phone-inventor-talks-of-first-cell-call/d /d-id/1109376.

PAGE 14

"The First Text Message Celebrates 25 Years," NPR, December 4, 2017, https://www .npr.org/2017/12/04/568393428/the-first-text -messages-celebrates-25-years.

PAGE 22

"Steve Jobs Introducing the iPhone at MacWorld 2007," YouTube, December 2, 2010, https ://www.youtube.com/watch/?v=x7qPAY9JqE4.

PAGE 24

John Callaham, "The History of Android OS: Its Name, Origin and More," Android Authority, August 18, 2019, https://www.androidauthority .com/history-android-os-name-789433/.

PAGE 27

"Siri Demo by Scott Forstall at Apple Special Event Oct. 4, 2011," YouTube, October 5, 2011, https://www.youtube.com/watch?v =SpGJNPShzRc.

GLOSSARY

CELLULAR: relating to a network in which a signal is transferred from one tower to the next

CLAMSHELL: a mobile phone that folds in half, with certain components in each half

COMMERCIAL: designed for sale and profit

DATA: information

DIGITAL: composed of electronic data

ENGINEER: a person who designs and builds complex machines, systems, or structures

LEAPFROG: to progress by keeping one unit in action while moving another unit past it

NETWORK: an interconnected system

OPERATING SYSTEM (OS): software that controls a computer, smartphone, or tablet

OPERATOR: a person who connects a caller to the person receiving the call

PERSONAL ASSISTANT: software that helps users with tasks

PORTABLE: able to be easily carried or moved from place to place

PROTOTYPE: a first experimental model of a device

RADIO WAVES: electromagnetic waves that travel through the air

TWO-WAY RADIO: a radio that can both transmit and receive radio waves and is used for person-to-person voice communication between users.

VOICE RECOGNITION: a system that can understand spoken commands

WEARABLE: a device that a person wears

LEARN MORE

Abramovitz, Melissa. *How Do Computers Talk to One Another?* Minneapolis: Lerner Publications, 2016.

How Stuff Works—How Smartphones Work
https://electronics.howstuffworks.com/smartphone1.htm

Kiddle—Telephone Facts for Kids
https://kids.kiddle.co/Telephone

Miller, Derek. *How Are Smartphones Made and Sold?* New York: Cavendish Square Publishing, 2019.

PCMag—Cell Phones for Kids: A Visual History
https://www.pcmag.com/feature/360716/cell-phones-for-kids-a-visual-history

Zoehfeld, Kathleen Weidner. *Phones Keep Us Connected.* New York: Harper, 2017.

INDEX